Poems
for a Small Park

E. D. Blodgett

AU PRESS

to all wayfaring strangers

Because these poems would never have seen the light of day without the help of many people, I want to thank warmly:

Gabriele Barry, Douglas Carlyle, and Linda Wedman for their encouragement;

Lin Zhong, who provided the Chinese poems;

Judy A Bear who provided the Cree poems;

Darlene Auger, who provided Cree syllabics with the help of Matilda Auger, Estheranna Stäuble, and Dorothy Thunder;

Esther Laurena Auger, who provided the poem in Michif;

Andrij Hornyatkevyc, who provided the poem in Ukrainian;

Patricia Godbout and Louise Ladouceur who reviewed the poems in French;

and especially my wife Irena, who took the photographs.

Habent sua fata libelli – books have their own destinies, and this book arose from the City of Edmonton's commission for the Louise McKinney Riverfront Park in downtown Edmonton. As a part of the park's design, the poems in this book are engraved on stainless steel plaques attached to lamp posts that light the promenade along the riverfront. The park is not the book, so you may wish to walk through the park and walk through these poems.

The poems were written originally in lucid English and French with occasional Cree, Michif, Chinese, and Ukrainian translations that speak to the unique multicultural ambience cultivated in Edmonton. Just as they do in the park, the poems in these languages come into view first as a way of showing respect to these cultures in the making of the city. The setting in most of the poems includes sharp Canadian imagery: "coyotes," "frozen fountains," "glaciers," and "poplars." Blodgett has most masterfully interwoven these essentially Canadian landscape images with the resilience and the pioneer spirit that define Canadians through the use of delicate tropes and figurative devices as when, for instance, he personifies Edmonton's "trees" which to him appear to "possess" "humility" and "braveness" "beneath the ice and wind and snow."

The lyrics are dense with powerful images and thoughtful metaphors that create memorable links between Canadian nature (even within city limits) and the sublime, which in Blodgett's poetry is used interchangeably with "silence" as heard outdoors mostly during wintertime. Blodgett incorporates "silence" and its everlasting and weighty presence on earth quite frequently in all his lyrics. The poet traces the origin of his preoccupation with silence to his interest in sacred texts and the fact that God in these texts has revealed to us that mankind was created from "nothing." "Nothing," according to Blodgett, is nothing but "silence." And God is silence, and all activities on earth are the outcome of the mysterious relationship and the interaction that exist between silences, Blodgett believes. The secondary silence that encompasses all nature and creatures, both animate and seemingly inanimate, originates from the primary silence that is the divine. All creatures carry within themselves this silence, but the more silent a creature is, the closer it is to the source. Based on this philosophical principle of Blodgett's ideology, stones and pebbles, which are lowest in the great chain of being, are closer to the sublime than any other creature because of their overwhelming silence.

Despite the deceptive simplicity of language and form in *Poems for a Small Park*, the lyrics almost always speak through metaphysically subtle ideas. In Douglas Barbour's words, the small lyrics, "in a sequence meant to be read as a whole . . . evoke place as possessing transcendental possibilities for the carefully perceiving eye." These lyrics are most certainly not silent themselves; they open small windows to the small park in downtown Edmonton and to silence itself.

Blodgett also believes that nature and natural elements are in a constant state of flux. The poet is of the opinion that the transience in nature can be easily perceived if one watches closely and with perceptive eyes. Change is the only stable and permanent ingredient in nature, and like silence, it encompasses all beings and all nature. Interestingly, Blodgett's lyrics speak to change by delicately and unconsciously forcing us to see natural phenomena around us in a different light each time we read his poems. By referring to the most ordinary phenomena in nature through poetry, Blodgett "washes the dust of custom from our eyes" as the Iranian contemporary poet, Sohrab Sepehri advises us to do regularly, and by so doing defamiliarizes them and refamiliarizes us with our environment and ourselves. As Sepehri says: "eyes should be washed; a different vision should be sought / words should be washed / words should be the wind itself; words should be the rain itself" – in an ongoing state of flux and passage, and only then we can truly "see" and this is precisely what these lyrics do: introducing us to the earth, to one another, and above all, to ourselves.

The philosophical nature of these poems does not make them inaccessible, however. These lovely short lyrics are written to be read by anyone. According to George Amabile, they "revive an awareness of our origins, our intimate confluence with the processes of earth, air, water, fire, stars, moon and cosmos. They remind us that this sense of other in ourselves reaches like light, or music, in all directions, back beyond history, and forward toward a hopeful but uncertain future." With their exquisite eloquence, these lyrics strike chords in us in response to nature and its elements. Graceful, and dressed in beautiful yet unpretentious apparel, Blodgett's sincere words appeal to us all and bring out our humanity in a most magical way.

– Manijeh Mannani, Edmonton, 2008

Dies aber läßt sich noch verschweigen
Wie gut das Gras ist und wie leis.

– Rainer Maria Rilke

Gifts of a River

beginnings just appear
so like a drowsy eye

suddenly awake
where a river wells up

uncoiling from the ice
where snug beside the land

it lay dreaming at
our feet in quiet sleep

ᐸᐯᕓᐦᑖᑲ
ᐅᐣᑭ ᒪᑐᕑᐣᑫˣ
ᒍᕁᓂ ᑭᑎᕓᕑᐁᐦᐅᐦᐊ·

ᐅᐦᑕᒐᑐᒐᐦᑿ
ᒪᒪᐣᑫᕝᐊ·ᐅ
ᐊᐦᐄᐦ ᑯᕁ ᐊᐦᑐᒐᐃᐊ·ᐅ

tread lightly on
the new grass
it is not ours

breathe in the air
with awe
it is the spirit's breath

pi aku´ pi ak   pa wa k´an
ki ihtamaka ta pimatisewin
nat a kam ta la riyver

ki itote maka ki kispanouhk
ekwa ka sēkc´ouwahk kakiyaw diloo
ta koc´ipaik

ka kiskac´wak ki kisipanouk
le mama ochi diloo
ekota sokkan ekwa ka kiki kanatan

un seul rêve
nous habitait le corps
le long de la rivière

celui d'aller au bout
et puiser toute cette eau
de sa source

de saisir enfin
la mère des eaux
dans sa pureté primesautière

10

as from beads of rain
the early light glances off
the wakened river toward

the dazzled children who
wait beside the bank
their eyes frozen fountains

but where is to be found
the dream of rivers exhaled
free from winter ice

in willow tufts perhaps
or the breath of clean birds
come back pursuing the sun

late in the afternoon
deer drift toward the bank
gazing with wakeful eyes

at houses that throughout
the day start to rise
as if the wind among the leaves

the river flowing past
had strangely come to rest
no farther place to reach

but swallows so swift
trace their curves across
the sky and close to banks

happy with the eaves
they find to shelter from
the ruthless noon-day sun

as if unmoved by sun
the shy retreats of deer
and birds in high suspense

the river dreams of its
descents yet to come
and never to be known

and as we walk here
let us remember them
whose dreams created in

the depths of human flesh
never rose in flight
but stood beside these shores

reaching with longing for
the other bank that rose
forever beyond their grasp

beauty from summer falls
unnoticed through ravines

that from the river reach
deeper through the earth

where silence unadorned
rises in our hands

the leaves that now fall here
have fallen here before

anyone knew that leaves
in such infinities fall

and how the heavens exhale
their long sighs of stars

transparent in the late
light that falls across
the river slowing down

every tree becomes
the perfect dream of trees
and there divinity

close to the end of day
silence on its knees
takes up residence

the last to find sleep
in the longer nights of fall

the coyotes fill the air
with sharp cries of glee

that summon stars and moon
the river suddenly

overcome with dreams
echoes of fading song

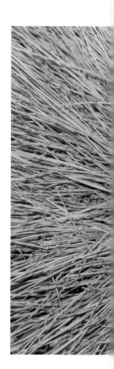

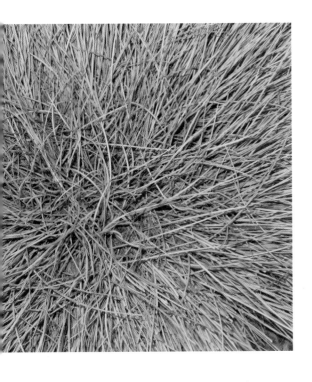

the time of legend falls
slowly on this place
everywhere unseen

but each return of snow
the moon settling on
the river like a leaf

composed of silence and
unfathomable light
are the only tales it tells

autant de fois
que tombent les feuilles
avons-nous flâné ici

pour les contempler
telles des rêves qui
flottent en dérive vers la mer

winter falls at length
through darkness and the snow
unable to go on

unable on the still
river to return
making this the last home

all elsewhere now
the dream that is to come
unable to take shape

now let us salute
all children who
never saw the light

and all mothers whom
winter took away
and all who have stood here

their names written in
the wind that falls without
a trace across the ice

and let us turn our heart
to old trees that through
the many winters of

their lives have reached forth
to greet the passing birds
and in their branches held

the winds that went astray
beneath the frozen moon
and solitary stars

quelqu'un dans l'obscurité
murmurait *adieu*

tel le son
de la rivière gelée

and so the last dream
is what the river dreams

asleep beneath the ice
of its invisible

descent from glaciers
beyond sight to seas

and where at last it wakes
soundless it disappears

Dreams of a City

ᐊᒪᓕᑫᐸᐧᐟ ᐱᑭᐦᐋᐸ᙮ᐄ
ᐊᓂᑫ ᑲᕆᕈᑲᐸᐸᐧᐅᐧᐣᑕᐦᑭᐧ
ᐊᓂᑌ ᑭᐦᒥ

ᐱᕆᐧᑯᐣᑫ×
ᒥᕆᐁᐧ᙮ ᐱᑭᐧᐅ
ᑲᑐᒫᐧᐨ ᐊᕈᐦᑎᐧᐊᑲᐧ×

ᐁᑫ᙮ ᒐᓂᑯᑊᐧ ᑲᐧᑭᕈᐊᐧᐅ
ᑲᐧᐣᐱᕆᕆᒣᒪᐣᐱᐅᐧ ᐅᑕ
ᑭᐱ ᒍᒐᐧᑲᐣᐅᐧ

nothing lay so clear
before those who stood
on these banks than the great

canopy of sky
that spread above them and
poured forth its endless light

and everything it seemed
stood eternal here
all that was laid bare

et tous qui ont suivi
sont entrés dans la lumière
comme si c'étaient une mer

qui les engloutissait
une mer pleine
de grands oiseaux

qui les menaient
plus profondément
vers la source des étoiles

or the golden light
of grain heading out
in summer calls them all

and gazing into it
they see summers spread
everywhere before

them flowing through the air
generations of
the sun standing in sheaves

while over all of them
the silent river and
the grass against their feet

a star unmoving stands
beyond anyone's grasp
this is the light that draws

them all into the dream
of what will be when they
no longer walk here

possibility
rises in the light

as if every dawn
turned departure toward

endless arrivals where
only the rising sun

holds time in its light
asleep upon our hands

but of the past of all
who stand here it is
somewhere other than now

intermittent in
the sky as if it were
the moon floating away

and all that is recalled
growing dimmer through
the evenings of the mind

so the river and the moon
turn around the star

that's fixed above our heads
their spell the larger light

that falls across this place
to enter it without

looking back where there
is nothing more to see

the one music that
resounds among these small
trees is elegy

for what is yet to be
looking toward the sun
and saying *goodbye goodbye*

everyone stands alone
upon the riverbank
gazing toward the stars

what gravity can hold
them there upon the sky
if not the great desire

that soars up to them
from this shore to theirs
to be at last at home

and hidden where the stars
are passing silently
across the cloudless sky

children are at play
unconcerned as if
they knew they were the dream

of children yet to be
playing already with
the past still to begin

other music falls
unheard across this place
but those who sense it know

that as it falls it falls
first from its final chord
and then unfolds until

at the end of night it seems
to have arrived at notes
that say *gather your breath*

and here begins all
opening in the first
light that unfailing

fills this place with its
stillness beyond name
spread out upon the least

pebble that lines the path
with its eternity
given to all who pass

not mountains nor the sea
but casual hills and bluffs
of poplars are our lot

invisible beside
us coyotes walk along
the margins of the night

their voices strangely filled
with sorrow and with joy
and all around them light

as if pouring from
their mouths not notes but stars
were falling brightly home

along horizons clouds
settle but only for
a moment then depart

the shapes that they assume
beyond what can be thought
as if children were

at play between the earth
and heaven's gate where they
are called to dance with stars

against the polar star
other lights arise

a fire floating through
the early winter sky

drawing the heart on
as if the only path

lay through ethereal
and open air where birds

alone scan all that lies
beyond as home enough

how brave the little trees
that have like sentinels

stood forever here
majesty is not

their lot or elegance
humility is all

that they possess beneath
the ice and wind and snow

speak tenderly of them
they wish no more of us

no ending may be found
in this place that takes

its bearings only on
the fixed star of the north

everything left behind
for that dream that brings

all that is into
that small space where grass

timeless and close to stars
returns to itself again

the path that leads
to paradise
is never straight

flowers alone
butterflies and snails
know the turns it takes

通往乐园
的路
唯蜗牛
曲曲弯弯
花与蝴蝶知道
其中沟沟坎坎

缓缓　徐徐

一粒粒挤压沉积

枯姜

泥土

大地腹内

当花园轮回

nothing sinks
so slowly as the ground
into itself

when gardens into
the womb of earth
return to die

танцюючи ми
прийшли на світ

найменший лист
танцює на своїй гілці

земля під нашими ногами
танцює через всесвіт

dancing we came
into the world

the least leaf
dances on its branch

the world beneath our feet
dances through the universe

© 2008 E. D. Blodgett

Published by AU Press, Athabasca University
1200, 10011 - 109 Street
Edmonton, AB T5J 3S8

Library and Archives Canada Cataloguing in Publication

Blodgett, E. D. (Edward Dickinson), 1935-
Poems for a small park / E. D. Blodgett.

(Mingling voices)
Issued also in PDF format.
ISBN 978-1-897425-33-6 (pbk.).–ISBN 978-1-897425-34-3 (pdf)

I. Title.

PS8553.L56P64 2008   C811'.54   C2008-907357-6

Cover and book design by Helen Adhikari
Printed and bound in Canada by AGMV Marquis

Please contact AU Press, Athabasca University at aupress@athabascau.ca
for permission beyond the usage outlined in the Creative Commons License.

A volume in the *Mingling Voices* series:
ISSN 1917-9405 (Print)
ISSN 1917-9413 (Online)